Jana B.

Falling Leaves

poetry collection

Jana B.

Falling Leaves

poetry collection

About the author:

Jana B. was born in Germany in August 2001. In November 2017, at the age of 16, she first started to upload her own poems on her instagram account @shadesofaseason. She still uses this platform to share her thoughts and to educate people on various topics, that belong to the wide spectrum of mental health.

Bibliografische Information der Deutschen Nationalbibliothek: Die Deutsche Nationalbibliothek verzeichnet diese Publikation in der Deutschen Nationalbibliografie; detaillierte bibliografische Daten sind im Internet über http://dnb.dnb.de abrufbar.

Herstellung und Verlag: BoD – Books on Demand, Norderstedt

ISBN: 978-3-7526-7183-4

Contents

Anticipation

I know that, if you knew me, you would expect me to be this "normal" and inconspicuous girl from next door, growing up with both of her parent in their own house.
No deeper issues.
Just inconspicuous.

If you're reading those words, you most likely experienced something that had a huge impact on you. For now, it doesn't matter whether it's been *positive* or *negative*, but we'll have a closer look on these terms later on anyways.

It doesn't matter if you grew up safe and sheltered or if your home never felt like one. We all experience things that we don't tell anyone about immediately or ever. Moreover it's so individually how much a certain situation affects us and our well-being. Just because something affected you, doesn't mean the same thing has to affect someone else in the same way, and the other way round.
That's why we should never judge someone for the way they deal with incidents, situations and feelings.
Everyone *handles* things differently.
Everyone *is* different.

But people still judge.
Especially the elderly, probably wouldn't really expect me to know a lot about the feeling of being broken, feeling exhausted, worthless and desperate.

-Not enough to write a book about it in particular-

But that's the point.
People always think they know you, because of what you show them.
They think they know how you think and feel.
Know who you are. Where you're going.
They judge you for everything you do.
For everything you do, that wasn't expected of them.

But I never show people every part of me. Most people only get the positive and happy part and they would - for sure - be surprised by reading those words. But I don't think you're any different. I mean it's normal not to share your deepest thoughts and feelings with everyone.

But
Do you even let yourself feel the "*bad*" feelings?
Do you know where you are going?
Do you know how to deal with your fears, thoughts and feelings *constructively*?
Do you have any idea, how you should start overcoming the feeling of being broken, exhausted, depressed and anxious?

This book isn't an instruction on how to overcome anxiety, depression, eating disorders or any other issues!
This book is the result of my own process and growth.
The poems are a collection of everything I wrote throughout the years of falling, breaking, recovering and most importantly - healing.

I decided not to only share the poems with you, but to give this book a special structure.
The *four* chapters build on each other and you should definitely read them in the right order. Every single chapter consists of the poems and also my intention behind the chapter! And you definitely need to read the intention to understand everything completely and to take something out of this book which helps you with your own recovery.

This book starts with a completely broken teenage girl, who feels lost, lonely and anxious.
It develops to a young woman who slowly gains back hope, strength and faith.
And eventually she will find her way to grow, rise, get better and slowly starts believing in her abilities.

SPOILER:
You're able to get there too :)

TRIGGER WARNING

The following contents might be triggering, since they deal with depression, anxiety, eating disorders and other topics. Especially the first chapter!

falling
(poems)

In your eyes,
I'm *alive*.
In your eyes
I'm *living*.
But the truth,
the ugly truth,
I'm just *existing*.
Full of doubts,
you'll never see,
'cause the facade,
keeps drowning me.
Keeps you thinking I'm alright.
Don't you know,
I'm *dying* inside.

been chosen last since I can think

The hunger,
the pain,
it all goes insane,
heavy thoughts,
happy front,
tell me how
it will go on.
Save me from these demons,
just wanna run away,
at the same time wanna stay,
not willing to let go
what lingers in my mind.

empty, but beyond the point of emptiness.

Empty.
Not able to feel.
the pain,
the frustration,
the anger,
anymore.
All what's left -
the silence
that keeps reminding,
what you *could be* today
but *you're not*,
you're *never* gonna *be*,
if you won't stand up,
and fight for finally getting
happy.

I can't fix this mess I'm making

feels like I just keep on breaking.

all the people on the ground
are those who smile the most
smile to hide all their pain
'cause
no one ever asks
no one knows their story
neither what they've gone through
and
they never will
'cause
all they do is judging.

I'm always there on time
'cause none of them would know
I'm missing.

I know that it's wrong,
but I just don't care.
Keep on committing this self-destructive
behavior.
It's only that I'm used to it.
Letting down myself and anyone else.
All I do is

pretending

lying

doubting

crying

although all I wanted was keep on
trying.

too much   to feel the heights
          gravity

how do I feel?
- a little lost.
I wanna talk
- but then I don't.
No one understands my burden
and they shouldn't take it too.

I wanna cry.
I wanna try.
Same time
just wanna deny,
everything I'm going through
and everything I'm feeling
too.

I care but I pretend I don't.

let coping hit another round.

the sun goes down - and so do you.
the light turns out,
now hit the blues,
with all these feelings
you've tried so hard
to hide the entire day.
they just appear,
the worst part is - they stay.

first tear drops onto the bedsheet,
only if you're lucky - just not too empty.
thoughts start going crazy,
that moment - there's just no end to see.

feeling lost.
feeling alone.
feeling like you can't move on.

suddenly
you're waking up
sleepless, tear-stained face
'cause you just couldn't stop.

just put yourself together
make it through another day
pretending you're totally
okay.

head's too full.
heart's too empty.

Pretending hurts.
Pretending everything's fine,
I'm fine.
Surviving days by wearing a mask,
I just don't want anyone to ask,
since I feel like they all expect way too much,
expect me to be alright,
like honestly most of the time.

So I'm
keeping this facade upright,
but still
all I want is to genuinely be alright.

again - I'm sitting here
feels like I keep hitting "repeat"
just stare at the ceiling
not really doing anything

am I alive or just existing?
is all of this ever gonna come to an ending?

when we meet up
you always act like you are bored
kinda supports my definition
of my own worth

Silence.
They say silence is silent.
But once you get hurt
you know it ain't the truth.

The silence of loneliness
It can be loud.
Unbearable loud.
All these voices are screaming.
Tryna shout you down.
Feels like there's no way out.
Breakdown.

falling
(intention)

falling - this chapter refers to quite a dark episode of my life or rather my youth. To be quite honest with you, it's not even that long ago, just maybe a year, not even two.

And I could tell you that I wished I never felt this broken and lost. But honestly, that would be a lie. And I know it may sound cliché but this time taught me a lot.

I was just a child when I first started to feel this way, maybe a little naive, but just trying to figure everything out.

That's literally the point.

At this age, all we do is trying to figure out.
Figure out who we are,
who we want to be,
what we want to be,
our place and role in this society.

We are extremely vulnerable at this time and we tend to believe and trust in the wrong things and people easily.

There were these first relationships that scared me, as I was totally insecure about myself.

I bet you also had toxic relationships, toxic friendships, bullying, family issues, maybe even abusive or traumatic experiences - it all just comes together and has its impact on us - during our most vulnerable episode of life. During a time, in which we are already insecure enough and all we actually need are people we can trust, that support us and got our back.

Everyone deals differently with these influences, as already written in the introduction. And some of these coping mechanisms are socially positively recognized, others are disapproved by society.

I mean it's obvious that self-harm is a destructive way of handling things, *but* that doesn't mean that it's "bad" in the first place.

All you're trying to do, is making yourself feel a little better and if self-harm fulfills this purpose, it can't be considered bad in the first place.

But the question you should ask yourself is, if harming yourself is something that'll help you healing and recovering from bad experience in the long run?

Think about that & continue reading :)

allowing
(poems)

So conscious about
everything.
Still not ready to change
a thing.

no smile to the crowd
no mask you use for fraud
could ever ensure your heart
that you're fine
when you're not

so stop lying to yourself
you're as vulnerable as anyone else
and it's okay to be broken for a while
as long as you'll get up again
to show yourself
that can do otherwise

none of you know the version of me.
the one that I let none of you see.

I am having hard times making sense
of all of this.
most times I get out of my head
and
get out of my mind.
I need to start
letting someone inside.

I am gonna *let myself fall*.
A couple of times.

how do you think you will get the heights
and feel them
when you won't let yourself feel the lows?

feelings want to be felt.
they don't care about whether you like them or not.

I keep on telling myself,
that I am trying hard,
that I am giving my best,
giving my all,
to improve myself,
to change the game,
to get happy.

But the truth is
I just keep on telling
myself this.
The truth is,
I found something
in the middle of this game,
that caught me,
made it hard to stop.
That made it hard to stop
destroying everything
I am.

Instead of *just telling* myself
to change
I should *actually start acting* to
change.

how much do you trust yourself?

was looking for control,
something to hold on to.
didn't notice right away,
this one thing turned to torture.
it's controlling me and my mind now,
but I gotta get out of it somehow.

I am gonna let myself
fail & discover
until I get there.

Instead of staying up all night
to tell myself I'm alright
I start to let me feel it all
give myself the trust that I require
start to unravel and to fulfill my desire.

I know your trust got abused a million times,
still I hope someday you can give someone a try.

all the daily struggles,
seemed so far away,
as you built your wall,
to hide your truly self

but once you recognized,
you're destroying just yourself,
in the world created,
by you -
to feel more safe

you gotta get out there,
the place that you fear,
but once you made the step,
you gonna feel whats life,
and not just take a breath,
to stay out there alive.

you need to let yourself feel it.
suppression only causes more issues.

it's not weak if you need to be held.

allow yourself to.
it's getting easier.

it takes strength to take the space that you need to heal.

not being enough,
not being able to beat it
not being able to let it go
is -
what scares me.

but letting it go,
also -
scares me.
it's weird how something that holds you back,
that destroys you,
your happiness,
your ambitions,
your passions,
can be hard to let go.

i'm scared of failing.
all of this.
but still
I start letting myself feel it.

denial won't lead to healing

.

allowing
(intention)

allowing - this phase is, in my opinion, the most important one of the whole process.
Don't get me wrong, every state of the process, which leads to growth and healing, has its own significance, but without the state of allowing, there can't be any beginning of healing.

If you don't allow yourself to feel everything your mind and body want you to feel and if you even try to suppress all the emotions and thoughts that you consider "negative", you'll only make things worse.

Everything in life, even the tiniest thought and feeling, has its right to just be there and to be felt. More importantly there's a reason that these emotions appear.

I spent way too much time questioning myself and judging myself for feeling these "bad" and "destructive" things, because I told myself I am not allowed to feel this way, because others got it worse and experienced worse than I did.
I thought I had no right to and wasn't valid of feeling just not good.

Society also plays a big role, since everyone expects you to just work. Continue the show, no matter how you feel because it must go on and you just don't have any right to destroy the perfect illusion that people want you to maintain.
They always make you feel bad for feeling.
Make you feel bad for being.
Make you feel inhuman for being human.

I've been trying to figure out what exactly got me to this point. For me, the cause and trigger was just a complete blur. Meanwhile things got a little clearer, but the more I found out about what caused the breaking, the more I realized that it's not really important to find out. I used to think that I immediately get better, once I know what exactly broke me.

Surprisingly, I *didn't*.

That's why I truly believe that the cause, of these emotions, isn't something you should care about in the first place. Finding out what caused and triggered the emotions, could help you to understand it a little better. Also it could be helpful to notice, if something similar is about to happen in the future. But ignorance isn't holding you back from healing, because you should concentrate about healing and getting better in the future, not waisting too much time on digging up the past.

Feelings won't leave, just because you're not facing them. They remain and they will make their way back into the foreground. So there's no use in suppressing emotions.

Who decides whether a feeling is
"good" or "bad"
"positive" or "negative"
"helpful" or "destructive"
anyways?

Things that might considered "bad", can have a good reason to be there, every thought and feeling has its reason and if you don't allow yourself to face it, it'll just get worse.

It's exhausting to let yourself feel it and to allow yourself to be broken for a while, when you've taught yourself that you're not allowed to show this part of you, for years.
Not even to yourself.
But it gets easier.
And trust me,
it's the only way to heal.

recovering
(poems)

I'm done fighting myself,
done thinking I'm less
than anyone else.
Stand up 'n rise
'stead of believing all those lies,
that I told myself long enough,
done thinking I'm not good enough.
It's all gonna be alright,
as soon as I'm changing the sides,
from slow suicides
'n self-destructive homicides
to some self-love and a
confident kind of mind.

I convinced myself to feel it.

insecure 'bout being me
standin' up for what I wanna reach
'bout things I do
sadly it's true
I'd love to show some confidence
which
society turned into arrogance
being judged for reaching my happy end
is what's holding back
right in this moment

take care your issues won't become your identity.

"i'm fine" I said a million times
with million of some other lies.

don't wanna talk
don't wanna cry
but still don't even wanna try.

it's a deadly game
in which we go insane.
let's start right now,
'cause we all know
we won't get better
unless we try.

all the time I was trying to be anyone but myself.
but why?

we live in a world
that is out to break us
any way it can.
but we can learn
how to handle things
differently.

today's gonna be the first day
of the rest of my life.

Feeling small,
nearly insignificant,
compared to the weight of the world.
Watch the time ticking,
passing by.

But you gotta try letting go,
those feelings and thoughts,
which let you pass the time,
without living.

Let them go,
be yourself
feel alive,
don't hold yourself down,
down deep in a hole,
feel the air,
the fresh breeze,
take a deep breath.
Be unstoppable.

just because you're hurting
doesn't mean I'm not.

We're all looking for someone to save us
&
we all have the urge to save the world.
But it's okay if we start by *saving* only one person
&
it's okay,
if this one person is
yourself.

It's not selfish.
It's necessary.
Necessary to be happy,
to feel fulfilled
&
loved.
Because
I truly believe
that you can't love someone else,
if you don't love
-at least accept-
yourself
first.

gaining back my faith and trust.

It's kinda funny,
how natural behaviors
turn into such a big deal.
Normal things turn into bad habits
&
you just can't tell how this really happened.
Just tryin' to figure out
a way to escape your own mind.
Running from the demons.
Trying so hard.
To get free.
To get happy.
To finally live again.

just because you're broken
doesn't mean you have to stay broken.

and when you feel like things get way to heavy
you gotta surround yourself with people
who bring out the best in you
who manage to distract you
who change your destructive thoughts
into more positive ones
and who can take away
parts of your anxiety.
your serious, but honestly so pointless
anxiety.
and eventually
you slowly learn
to let go of it.

feels so good to feel again.

And all the sudden,
we slip into adulthood,
which feels like a change
without prior warning.
Yesterday
we were kids,
without the responsibility,
life throws on us.
Now
we need to take care
of ourselves.
Need to show the world
what we've got
&
what we are willing to give.

If you really wanted, I could let you inside.

You're enough.

You're enough to get you out of this place.
This place full of darkness,
self-destructive thoughts.

You're enough to walk away.
Walk away from all the people
who wanna see you fail,
over and over again.

You're enough to be allowed.
Be allowed to live a life *you* want,
no one else.

You're enough to be allowed.
be allowed to do whatever *you* want.

Even if you think you don't deserve it.
Even if you think you're not worth it.
Even if you think you didn't.
Let me tell you one thing.

you are enough.

You still think I got it all figured out?
All of the times, I spent not being me.
I hope now you know, it's not always happy.

It's already been a while now,
I slowly start to figure it out somehow.
I've got nothing left to hide
gonna let you all inside.
Tell you all the things that I didn't want told
I'm learning to stop acting so cold.

I'm sorry, but the wisest thing you can do,
is joining your own team.

all the white lies
all of these walls
they're all starting to fall
I'm gonna let myself try
and I'm not gonna stop

it's totally fine not to be there, yet.
'cause in time, I'll be fine.

recovering
(intention)

recovering - the most important thing you need to know about this state is, that it takes so much time.

There's absolutely no use in wanting to rush things and and being impatient.
There's something that really hurt you back then and it takes so much longer to heal and recover than it takes to break.
It's just like earning money and spending money, the latter is much faster :)

You might be asking yourself why you have to go through this in the first place. My answer is probably not satisfying to you, but I think that we all have to go through bad times, to even notice the good times or rather to appreciate the good. Sometimes we get so caught up in our routines and don't notice what we've got, until it's gone.

But it's okay if recovery is too difficult to handle sometimes, even to give up or relapse. Giving up is not usually associated with *strength* and *healing* by society, which is literally so wrong.
Sometimes we need to let go of things to find new perspectives, to see that the way we chose isn't the proper way for us, even if it's the best way for somebody else. Also giving up and relapsing can show us how far we got, because we first start to notice, when we fell back again. But we already know how we once got there and we can always go back and use everything we already learned, to heal further.

Society always wants us to work, to be perfect and strong. But these beliefs are so misleading.

Everything is a lesson.
Everything has a reason.

Recovery is a long process filled with doubts, anxiety and relapses.
The more you face them, the stronger you get.

growing
(poems)

still-
not wanna
show up first,
sometimes-
still doubting
my own worth.

but-
not recidivistic
anymore,
when-
old habits knock
on my door.

and-
learned how to cope
with feels constructive,
not-
gonna end it
self-destructive.

it's-
always a huge
up 'n' down
that-
doesn't mean
I haven't grown.

it's all about the peaks and valleys.

growth takes peace.
peace takes time.

growing can either mean to act a little warmer,
also to act a little colder.

...

...
you need to be able to say "no".
self-care isn't selfish.

If you get things wrong,
you'll hear it.

If you get things right.
You won't hear it.

That's just society.
I don't get it.

Why always telling people what they've got wrong,
instead of telling 'em
what they've been doing great?

Why always tearing others down,
instead of motivate, praise & support?

Be different.

Be one of those who build other people up,
be kind and supportive.

growing
(intention)

growing - first to mention: you don't have to be fully recovered to start growing.
Growing means development and comes with a lot of struggles and challenges that you have to face and they are most likely going to feel uncomfortable.
But I often read the quote
"Great things never came from comfort zones"
and I totally agree with that, because if you always do what feels good and comfortable, you would never try new things, never get new perspectives, never explore new and unexpected things.

What's the worst that could happen, when you try new things?
Getting judged?

There will always be people who will judge and who won't be happy for your successes and accomplishments.
There will always be people who would rather see you to be torn apart and almost on the ground.

But that shouldn't stop you from doing what you love, from doing what you want and from doing what you're good at.

People keep judging you because they are either envious or they just don't like what you're doing, but that's not your problem.

It's funny how we kind of believe, that we can postpone things, that we want to do and try someday, endlessly. As if we are undying, as if we are immortal.

Do not, do not do things, just because you're scared of what others might think or because you're scared of failing.

Growing isn't equal with perfection.

You could start by changing a tiny thing in your daily routine and practice gratitude to appreciate what you already got even more.
I promise you, that your mindset will slowly change. Slow, but still.

Falling Leaves
(intention)

falling leaves - I was looking for a title ever since I knew that I'm gonna write a book, out of all the poems that I wrote. But I just couldn't find one that's catchy and ambiguous.
I wanted something that you look at and immediately wonder what's behind.

Falling leaves has so many different meanings to me.

First of all, the word *fall* (like *autumn)* is included.
If you know me at least a little, you might know that autumn is by far my favorite season of the year.
Fall has several meanings, which are more profound than you would assume at first.
It can be seen as change, teach us to be more present and it radiates a certain coziness.
The only thing that is constant in life, is change.
The whole nature changes during autumn and so do our minds, bodies and everything that surrounds us.
Everything is constantly developing.
We could use that knowledge to practice to live more presently and appreciate what we got, before it's gone.

Moreover the leaves that are falling down, the temperature which is falling, are the proof that letting go doesn't always have to be bad. It can lead to something new, something great(er).
It's worth trying.

But *falling leaves* can also be read as "falling stops".
My first chapter is called "falling" and throughout the course of the book, the first chapter gradually fades into the background and starts to play a minor role.

German Poems
(bonus)

(diese Poems sind auf Deutsch, wurden aber ganz zu
Beginn verfasst, im "falling" Kapitel)

Zu viel,
zugleich,
zu wenig.
Renn' im Kreis
und dreh' mich.
Der ganze Scheiß,
zu hoch der Preis.
Will drüber reden,
doch trau' mich nicht.
Mauern zu hoch,
für's volle Gewicht.

Warte d'rauf
das jemand kommt,
der all das
wieder hinbekommt.

Gefühl' zu stark
zum Auseinandersetzen,
versuch' immer wieder,
mich ihm zu widersetzen.

Zeitgleich so leer,
einfach zu schwer,
zu beschreiben was in mir ist
- was mit mir ist -
all das was mich immer weiter frisst.

Auslöser - hin oder her,
der Kopf so voll,
das Herz so leer,
nun sitz' ich hier,
es geht nichts mehr.

Frag' mich wann ich aufhören kann,
zu versichern ich käm' allmählich an.
Bin allein,
doch eigentlich nicht,
einzig und allein Schuld bin ich.

Stoß' alle weg
nicht gut genug,
um ihnen zu zeigen was in mir ruht.
Zweifel, Angst, Melancholie,
weiß nicht wieso,
doch es tut weh.

Ein
- halt -
Zwei,
Augenblick'.
Mehr brauch' ich eigentlich nicht,
um mich zusammenzureißen,
auf all meine Gefühle zu scheißen.
Doch will ich noch?

Wie lang kann ich's noch durchzieh'n?
Mit Dauer-Lächeln durch's Leben zu zieh'n?
Hab' genug von mir selbst,
und all den falschen Glaubenssätzen,
die ich mir weiterhin erzähl'.
Bin gleich viel wert
wie jeder hier
oder auch nicht - sag du es mir.

Und nun?
Nun sitz' ich hier,
frag' mich "was ist passiert"
All' die Träume, Pläne, Ziele,
mit funk'len Augen als Kind kreiert.
Ungeduld die Welt zu erobern
zu zeigen wofür wir stehn'
Und ich frag' mich,
wo ist all dies geblieben?
Wo sind die Träume, Pläne, Ziele?
Gefangen in Gedanken,
in Angst, Melancholie.
Angst davor zu sein,
zu verlieren,
nachzugeben.
Angst davor -
aufzugeben.